THE DAYS OF NOAH

tate publishing
CHILDREN'S DIVISION

Published by Tate Publishing & Enterprises, LLC
127 E. Trade Center Terrace | Mustang, Oklahoma 73064 USA
1.888.361.9473 | www.tatepublishing.com

Tate Publishing is committed to excellence in the publishing industry. The company reflects the philosophy established by the founders, based on Psalm 68:11,
"The Lord gave the word and great was the company of those who published it."

Illustrations by http://www.maaillustration.com

Published in the United States of America

ISBN: 978-1-63063-051-5
1. Religion
2. Family And Relationships
13.10.17

When God looked upon the earth,
What did He see?
But evil and violence
From men constantly.

God said, "I'll destroy
The earth I created.
For now I am sorry
I ever have made it."

Genesis 6:5-7 The Lord saw that the wickedness of man was great on the earth, and that every intent of the thoughts of his heart was only evil continually. The Lord was sorry that he had made man on the earth, and He was grieved in His heart. The Lord said, "I will blot out man whom I have created from the face of the land, from man to animals to creeping things and to birds of the sky; for I am sorry that I have made them."

But one man alone
To the mind of God came.
He was good, he was righteous,
He called God by name.

So God said to Noah,
"An ark you shall build.
The earth will be flooded.
Mankind will be killed."

Genesis 6:8-9,13-14 But Noah found favor in the eyes of the Lord. Noah was a righteous man, blameless in his time; Noah walked with God. Then God said to Noah, "The end of all flesh has come before Me; for the earth is filled with violence because of them; and behold, I am about to destroy them with the earth. Make for yourself an ark of gopher wood; you shall make the ark with rooms, and cover it inside and out with pitch."

"This ark will hold you and your family and kin.
Then animals, birds, and all things will come in.
They'll come male and female, to keep them alive,
And gather much food, for that's how you'll survive."

Genesis 6:18-19,21 "I will establish My covenant with you; and you shall enter the ark – you and your sons and your wife, and your sons' wives with you. And of every living thing of all flesh, you shall bring two of every kind into the ark, to keep them alive with you; they shall be male and female. As for you, take for yourself some of all food which is edible, and gather it for yourself; and it shall be food for you and for them.

Noah to save him, his wife, and his kin,
Not knowing the day that the rain would begin,
Believing that God would be true to His word,
Began building the ark, just as he had heard.

Hebrews 11:7 By faith Noah, being warned by God about things not yet seen, in reference prepared an ark for the salvation of his household.

Its width fifty cubits, its height thirty tall,
Three hundred in length, Noah measured them all.
With a door on the side and a window on top,
They'd stay safe and dry, till the rain God would stop.

Genesis 6:15-16 (God said) "This is how you shall make it: the length of the ark three hundred cubits, its breadth fifty cubits, and its height thirty cubits. You shall make a window for the ark, and finish it to a cubit from the top; and set the door of the ark in the side of it; you shall make it with lower, second, and third decks."

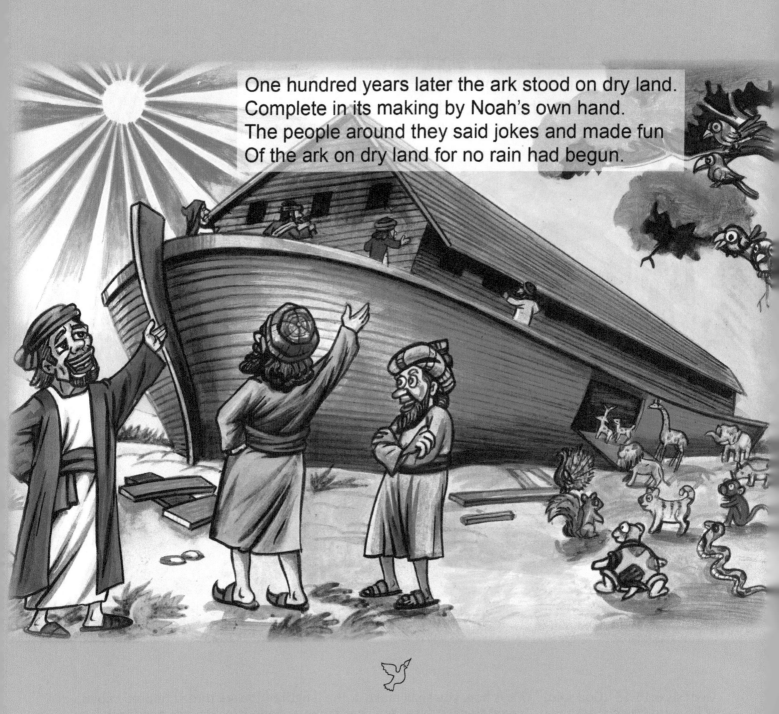

One hundred years later the ark stood on dry land.
Complete in its making by Noah's own hand.
The people around they said jokes and made fun
Of the ark on dry land for no rain had begun.

Genesis 6:22 Thus Noah did; according to all that God had commanded him, so he did.

Then God spoke again,
"The time is now nigh.
In seven more days
I will open the sky."

"Forty days, forty nights,
I will send down the rain.
All creatures will die.
Those with you will remain."

Genesis 7:1,4 Then the Lord said to Noah, "Enter the ark, you and all your household; for you alone I have seen to be righteous before Me in this time. For after seven more days, I will send rain on the earth forty days and forty nights; and I will blot out from the face of the land every living thing that I have made."

Noah, his wife, his three sons and their spouses,
to follow God's plan they left all of their houses.
They entered the ark, for to God they were true.
Then they watched as the animals came two by two.

Genesis 7:13 On the very same day Noah and Shem and Ham and Japheth, the sons of Noah, and
Noah's wife and the three wives of his sons with them, entered the ark.

The lions and elephants, bears and baboons,
The tigers and panthers, the skunks and raccoons.
The deer and the horses, the bison, the boar,
The sheep and the goats and the foxes and more.

Genesis 7:14 They and every beast after its kind, and all the cattle after their kind.

The turtles and lizards and crocodiles too,
The python, the boa, and when they were through,
The robins and blue jays, the dove and the lark
And all kinds of birds then flew into the ark.

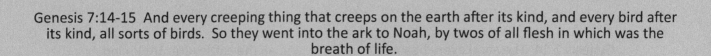

Genesis 7:14-15 And every creeping thing that creeps on the earth after its kind, and every bird after its kind, all sorts of birds. So they went into the ark to Noah, by twos of all flesh in which was the breath of life.

Then God, reaching down with His hand, shut the door,
Those in would be saved and those out were no more.
The fate of each man had been sealed by God's hand.
But those on the outside did not understand.

Genesis 7:16 Those that entered, male and female of all flesh, entered as God had commanded him;
and the LORD closed it behind him.

Matthew 24:39 And they (the evil men) did not understand until the flood came and
took them all away.

For seven more days the rain did not come.
The men on the land thought that Noah was dumb.
They married and drank and they partied all day.
They laughed and made fun as they went on their way.

Matthew 24:38 For in those days before the flood they were eating and drinking, marrying and giving in marriage, until the day that Noah entered the ark.

Genesis 7:10 It came about after the seven days, that the water of the flood came upon the earth.

Then lightning and thunder
And dark clouds did loom.
The men on the outside
Now knew of their doom.

They cried out to Noah,
"Please let us come in."
But they were destroyed
Due to violence and sin.

Genesis 7:11,21-22 In the six hundredth year of Noah's life, the fountains of the great deep burst open, and the floodgates of the sky were opened. All flesh that moved on the earth perished, birds and cattle and beasts and every swarming thing that swarms upon the earth, and all mankind; of all that was on the dry land, all in whose nostrils was the breath of the spirit of life, died.

Forty days, forty nights, the rain it did fall.
The earth was a flood. There was no land at all.
As waters rose higher the ark stayed afloat.
Though rocked to and fro, they were safe in that boat.

Genesis 7:17,19 The flood came upon the earth for forty days, and the water increased and lifted up the ark, so that it rose above the earth. The water prevailed more and more upon the earth, so that all the high mountains everywhere under the heavens were covered.

Then the fountains of deep and the floodgates up high
Were closed so no more of the rain could get by.
The waters went down as the rain it did stop.
After months could be seen the mountains on top.

Genesis 8:1-2,5 But God remembered Noah and all the beasts and all the cattle that were with him in the ark; and God caused a wind to pass over the earth, and the water subsided. Also the fountains of the deep and the floodgates of the sky were closed, and the rain from the sky was restrained. The water decreased steadily until the tops of the mountains became visible.

So a dove Noah sent from the ark as a test,
To see if the bird could find some place to rest.
The dove came back empty for no place was found,
A suitable spot for her feet on the ground.

Genesis 8:8-9 The he (Noah) sent out a dove from him to see if the water was abated from the face of the land; but the dove found no resting place for the sole of her foot, so she returned to him into the ark, for the water was on the surface of all the earth.

Again the dove searched
After seven more days,
And brought back an olive leaf
Found off a ways.

Now more and more water
Receded until,
A year had gone by,
They were on that boat still.

Genesis 8:10-11,13 So he waited yet another seven days; and again he sent out the dove from the ark.
The dove came to him toward evening, and behold, in her beak was a freshly picked olive leaf. So Noah
knew that the water was abated from the earth. Now it came about in the six hundred and first year,
the water was dried up from the earth.

Then God said to Noah, "You must disembark.
The land is now dry, so get off of that ark."
The door on the side of the ark opened wide.
All those from within could now step outside.

Genesis 8:15-16 Then God spoke to Noah, saying, "Go out of the ark, you and your wife and your sons and your sons' wives with you."

Then God said, "Be fruitful and multiply and,
I'll not curse the ground nor destroy those on land.
Seedtime and harvest, the seasons, the day,
The night, and the cold and the heat will all stay."

Genesis 9:1 And God blessed Noah and his sons and said to them, "Be fruitful and multiply, and fill the earth."

Genesis 8:21-22 And the Lord said to Himself, "I will never again curse the ground on account of man, and I will never again destroy every living thing, as I have done. While the earth remains, seedtime and harvest, and cold and heat, and summer and winter, and day and night shall not cease."

A covenant was made for all creatures and men.
The waters would not flood the earth, not again.
After the rain a bow sets in the sky.
It reminds God and men of the promise on high.

Genesis 9:12-13 God said, "This is the sign of the covenant which I am making between Me and you and every living creature that is with you, for all successive generations; I set My bow in the cloud, and it shall be a sign of a covenant between Me and the earth."

When you see a rainbow
Set high in the sky,
A sign of the covenant
Of ages gone by,

Remember that God
To His word will be true.
So if you follow Him
He will also save you.

Genesis 9:14-15 "It shall come about, when I bring a cloud over the earth, that the bow will be seen in the cloud, and I will remember My covenant, which is between Me and you and every living creature of all flesh; and never again shall the water become a flood to destroy all flesh."

CPSIA information can be obtained at www.ICGtesting.com
Printed in the USA
LVOW02s1008220414

382691LV00005B/13/P